A Choice Theor

Parenting

The Art of Raising Great Children

Nancy S. Buck Ph.D.

From the "Choice Theory in Action Series"

ISBN: 9781071426142

Dedication

With sincere love and thanks, I dedicate this book to all my children:

My son Paul and his wife Julie, and their two sons, Malakai, and Wyatt.
My son David and his wife Julianne, and their daughter Caelyn.

Since the day my identical twins were born they have taught me about the most important, challenging and rewarding job of my life — parenting. I never could have learned, written and taught so much about parenting without these remarkable, kind young men.

I also had no idea when I started this parenting journey that there would come a day when I would be someone's mother-in-law and potential worst nightmare. Can you imagine having a mother-in-law who calls herself a parenting expert?

I have been blessed with two remarkable daughters-in-law who with grace, good humor and love are the best and most perfect mothers for my grandchildren. We all know that at home I am Granma and nobody's expert on anything.

And to the worlds best grand babies! I always heard you never really know how large your heart can become until you have grandchildren. Now I know exactly what that means. Grand-parenting is all about love and fun. When other issues arise it's the perfect time for these kiddos to go home to Mom and Dad.

Parenting is my greatest joy and blessing!

CONTENTS

The Choice Theory In Action Series

This is one of a series of short books aimed at helping people gain better control of their lives using ideas from Choice Theory psychology, a theory of human behaviour that was developed by Reality Therapy creator Dr. William Glasser.

In this selection of books we explain the application of Choice Theory psychology to a range of popular themes such as   Addiction, Anger, Depression, Happiness, Parenting, Relationships, and Stress. The authors are all experts in Choice Theory psychology and all have studied directly under its creator, Dr. William Glasser.

Dr. Nancy S. Buck has created her "Peaceful Parenting" program based on Choice Theory and is the author of several books on parenting.

Hopefully this particular book will provide parents in particular with new insights and good advice on how to be better parents and to enjoy the wonderful challenge of bringing up their children.

Brian Lennon
Series Editor

Acknowledgments

More than forty years ago as an undergraduate in my psychiatric rotation for the nursing program, I was required to read a book and complete a book report. Knowing I had this assignment I reviewed the many books on my father's book shelves. He recommended I read the book Reality Therapy, written by William Glasser, MD. I chose that book using typical college student criteria; it was relatively short, had big print, and since my father owned the book, I had easy access.

That began my relationship with Dr. William Glasser and all the thousands of people I have met, learned from, learned with, taught, traveled and laughed with, and with whom I continue to make my emotional and intellectual home.

My sincere thanks and appreciation to Dr. Glasser and all these many people around the globe who share my filter of seeing the world from a Choice Theory psychology perspective. I feel privileged to have made this connection and association so early in my life. I know my life would have been very different without you, all my Glasser friends. I am blessed to be among the Glasser Groupies on the planet.

I'd like to give special thanks to two Glasser friends:

Susan A McGregor, "Sam," who carefully and lovingly edited this manuscript. If you've ever done any writing you know that your editor determines what kind of writer you will be. Thank you Sam for making this book so much better.

Brian Lennon, a generous, fun and funny friend came up with the brilliant idea to put together a book series on the application of Choice Theory psychology to every day living.   Thank you sincerely Brian for including me in this group of writers, and for acknowledging my contribution to Choice Theory psychology.

Introduction

The phone kept ringing and ringing, refusing to stop. I tried to ignore it, snuggling deeper beneath my covers. Didn't they know I was sick? Finally I surrendered, wrapped myself in a flannel cover and found the phone.

"Hello."
"Is this Dr Buck?"
"Yes."
"Oh Dr. Buck, I'm so glad to speak with you," said the caller with a very thick Brooklyn accent. She continued quickly without pause.

"My name is Shirley Jones. I was just on a flight from Boston to Miami. There was a mother with her young son on the flight with us. While we all were waiting to board the plane this little boy was behaving so poorly. Honestly, he was one of the worst behaved children I have ever seen; everyone was talking about it.

"Then I watched that mother calmly go over to her son, and asked him to sit next to her so she could start talking to him. That's all she did. No yelling, raised voices, threats or crying. It was a miracle.

"That little fellow calmed right down, and politely boarded the plane with her. He remained well behaved for the entire flight. I couldn't believe my eyes. It was a miracle!

"I just had to know what was going on. So I went right over to that young woman and asked her what she did. Do you know what she told me?"

Of course, now I was curious.

"No, what did she tell you?"

"She told me that she was doing 'Peaceful Parenting' and that she learned it from you! I knew immediately I needed to get in touch with you."

Suddenly the summer illness that had flattened me for the last five days was completely forgotten. This woman was so impressed by a mother who was practicing my Peaceful Parenting ideas that she had tracked me down and called me. Wow.

My lovely caller continued.

"I have this wonderful grandson. He really is a terrific child, but sometimes he gets a little aggressive. I could use your help. Do you think you could help him? Could you teach me how to help him?"

Twenty years have passed since that remarkable grandmother reached out asking me to help her. She wanted to know how to guide her grandson, and help her do it in a way that did not destroy their relationship in the process. Learning and applying the ideas of Choice Theory psychology to parenting helps parents learn to do just that.

This book is one in a series of short books about what motivates you and your behavior, as well as your child and her behavior, using the ideas from Choice Theory psychology developed by Dr. William Glasser.

Applying Choice Theory ideas to parenting is especially challenging. Parents want and feel obligated to guide, and teach their children to do right, be right and have everything right. Parents want children to be safe, successful and happy. Most people only know how to accomplish these goals using external control, meaning trying to force them to do what you want.

Amazingly, infants teach their parents the error of this. You cannot make a baby sleep when you think she should, or eat when he is not hungry. But as the infant grows into a baby, then a toddler, you forget this important lesson. Now you attempt to guide using externally controlling behaviors, including rewarding and punishing, all to try and get your child to do what you think she should, when you think she should.

Spend time with a pre-toddler to get a clear picture of the truth of Choice Theory psychology. He attempts to stand and lets go of his support, trying to find his balance. Inevitably he falls. Then what happens? He tries to stand again, and he falls again. He repeats this process over and over. Ultimately he succeeds.

Not once does a parent need to incentivize this "failing" child by offering a reward, or bribe to get the child to try standing again. The child is internally motivated to follow this essential biological genetic instruction. All human beings are born with the urge to stand and walk. Parents do not need to interfere by rewarding or punishing. Good parenting involves getting out of your child's way and letting him learn to do what he is biologically and genetically driven to do. Your child needs to try and fail, try again and fail again until ultimately he tries and succeeds.

This same process plays out in many everyday situations. Imagine your child completing her homework assignments or chores without your resorting to rewards, bribes, reminders or threats. Or respecting and following agreed upon curfews and responsibly caring for his personal possessions without you incentivizing. In the beginning there will be some attempts, failures and falling down. Through your support and guidance your child will get up and try again until ultimately he succeeds.

Parents are responsible for teaching and guiding children from infancy through childhood and into young adulthood. And yes, the task is daunting. When you choose to give up the usual attempts to influence through rewarding and punishing and replace this with the principles of Choice Theory psychology, the process becomes fun, and full of positive adventures and discoveries.

This does not mean there will never be a challenge or tension. But angry disappointment and disapproval are replaced with love and the desire to work together to figure out how to resolve these disagreements in ways that satisfy everyone.

I offer you this book so you can begin learning and implementing these parenting ideas right now. You will discover how to improve your family and improve your world!

1. The Basic Needs that Drive Behavior

Key Points:

- *Children are internally motivated to meet psychological needs.*
- *Children's behavior can be influenced but not controlled.*
- *People behave to meet their needs for safety, love, power, fun, and freedom.*

At the end of the last century William Glasser, MD, introduced Choice Theory psychology which offers a very different way of understanding human behavior and motivation. The ideas of Choice Theory are not hard to learn but are challenging to apply.

Choice Theory states that human beings are internally motivated. The outside world gives people information, but children and parents decide what to do, or not do, based on what is going on inside them at the time.

So when you ask your 7-year old to come inside for supper, your child hears your request as information. One child might decide to run inside as you asked because she is very hungry. Another child might decide to play one more inning of kick ball with his friends. Yes, he heard your request. Yes, he wants to eat supper. But he also wants to play one more inning because it's his turn to kick and he is sure he will kick the winning run!

Despite what you may have learned, children cannot be manipulated or controlled to behave just as parents want them to. Unfortunately there is a lot of information in our culture that would lead parents to believe they can, should, and must, control their children.

The reality is that people are not easily controlled. In fact the very urge to control others usually result in others resisting. If people were as easily manipulated and controlled as our culture represents, you too would be easily controlled and manipulated.

Do you have the ability to resist buying everything that is advertised to you through the media? Of course you do! No one is actually making you buy anything; you decide because you need or want a specific item, not because of the enticement of advertising.

Do you have the ability to resist your child's unhealthy or inappropriate requests? Even if your child tells you she "hates you" or "won't love you any more if you don't give her what she wants" you still have the ability to stick by your decision and answer with a firm "no." No matter how hard your child tries to externally control you, you can still make your own, internally driven decision.

Why do you think it's different with your children? Simply because they're smaller, less experienced and younger does not mean they are any more easily controlled or manipulated using external rewards and punishments.

Choice Theory psychology explains that your children are internally motivated, and parenting using Choice Theory psychology means you understand that you are also internally motivated. Both parents and children are born with the urge to control one another because parents and children are both born with the urge for power. Luckily you are also born with an urge for love. Your desire to stay connected with one another hopefully overcomes your desire to win and control each other. Using Choice Theory is more challenging than trying to control your children using external control ideas, but it is also more respectful of your child's capacity to learn and become a responsible adult. Ultimately this is more effective and rewarding for both parents and children.

All behavior, from birth until death, is motivated by genetic instructions. People experience these instructions as an urge to behave.

Many of the genetic instructions are biological, such as the urge to eat, breathe, eliminate, behave sexually and seek shelter.

People also are born with psychological genetic instructions. These urges drive people's behaviors so they feel safe and secure, feel loved and connected, feel powerful and in charge, laugh, learn and have fun, and feel free, and able to make choices. All human behavior, from birth to death is an attempt to meet your needs for safety, love, power, fun, and freedom.

Take a moment to reflect. What need or needs are you attempting to meet as you read this book? The answer is individual and can only be accurately answered by you. But a reasonable guess is that you're hoping this book will help you become a better, more effective parent. That translates into helping you meet your need for power. It's also possible that the reason you're reading this book is because your spouse, sister or friend recommended it, and you hope to stay connected to that person, meeting your need for love and belonging. Or perhaps you're beginning to feel like the choices you're making are not helping you deal with your present parenting dilemma. You're seeking more choices and alternatives, thus meeting your need for freedom. Or maybe you're stuck in a room where there is nothing else available to read other than this book. You're hoping for some distraction, entertainment, or fun to alleviate your boredom.

Whatever your answer, you are internally motivated to do what you are doing now. And as long as you are satisfying one of more of these needs, or you believe that eventually your needs will be met, you will continue reading the book. On the other hand, if this book is not satisfying any of your needs, and you don't believe it will in the future, you will close the book and stop reading it.

Everything your child is doing now is an attempt to meet her need for safety, love and belonging, power, fun or freedom. Let's see how this works.

What is your child doing now? Sleeping to meet his biological need for rest? Meeting his need for fun by playing hide-and-go seek instead of getting ready for bed as you asked? Or perhaps he's trying to meet his need for freedom so he can stay up longer and play rather than go to bed to sleep?

Say that your child needs more fun, and he doesn't think sleeping will provide it so he refuses to go to bed. You want your child to go to bed, and get to sleep so he is rested. Your need is power to ensure your child will follow your directions, get to bed and stay healthy.

Imagine making a game where your child can play to meet his need for fun. This new game involves him ultimately getting into bed, settling down and falling asleep. You both get what you want and need!

Can you imagine such a game? Here's one idea that might work. Make up a pretend story:

The floor is an ocean filled with sharks ready to eat anyone in the water. To be safe your child needs to get into bed quickly and stay there! Suddenly a large wave enters the room, threatening to wash everyone out of the boat-bed. We all must seek shelter by getting under the bedding with just our faces peeking out. As we peek out we see that the wave was made by a friendly giant whale who has chased all the sharks away. The whale wants to listen to the bedtime story that Dad is getting ready to read. Shall we let him stay?

Parenting using Choice Theory as your guide means learning what your child needs, becoming conscious of what you need, and figuring out how to combine the two in ways where you both get what you need and want responsibly and respectfully. Changing the way we do things is challenging in the short term, but step by step you will better understand and parent differently. And the result is a closer, more loving relationship with your child.

Practice Tips

For now start by observing and identifying the basic needs driving your child's and your own behavior.

Make a list of the needs below. Post it on your refrigerator door, an index card, your phone, or where ever you can see it regularly.

SAFETY   LOVE
POWER   FUN
FREEDOM

Start observing your child and guess what need is driving her present behavior.

Keep a journal listing the child's name, and your guess at the need driving her.

Your journal will be used to help you learn, remember and keep track.

If you have more than one child you can either focus on only one child per week or per day. Or you can focus on one child in this moment and a different child in the next moment. Just be sure you keep track of it in your journal.

Observe yourself and guess what need you are attempting to meet.

In your journal list your own name and write down the behavior and the need you guess is driving your present behavior.

The more you practice, the more familiar you will become with each of the basic needs as well as making the connection between behaviors and the internal needs motivating and driving them. You can do this with anyone, stranger or friend.

Don't worry about getting the right or wrong answer with the need; is this power or freedom? Is this fun or love? For now just guess at connecting an observable behavior and an unseen, internal genetic drive.

2. The Urge to Control Your Child

Key Points:

- *Parents want to keep their children safe, secure and alive*
- *Children are driven to be free to explore themselves and the world*
- *There is an inherent conflict between parents and children beginning pre-birth*
- *Parenting peacefully means teaching your children to be safe while you honor their need to be free*

I've had the good fortune to meet parents from all over the world. Not surprisingly most parents have the same quality world picture, (also known as hopes, dreams and desires) for their children. Almost all parents want their children to grow up to be happy, healthy, responsible adults who contribute to society and maintain a loving relationship with their parents.

Underneath this quality world picture there is another desire. All parents want their children to stay alive growing and maturing into adulthood. This urge is not unique to humans, it's shared by all mammals on the planet.

As soon as people realize they are going to become parents, whether biologically or otherwise, they begin worrying about the health and development of their unborn child.

This parental quality world picture of the health, well being and safety of children, both before and after birth, is so powerful that it effects virtually all parental decisions during the child's lifetime. This biological instinct is where a parent's urge to control their child comes from.

When first time parents of newborns leave their baby in the care of someone else, they become fearful and hesitant to leave. A baby monitor becomes a necessary nursery item. Parents of two-year olds become concerned that their child isn't eating enough, not nearly as much as the child ate six months ago. Then come worries about their preschooler being invited on a playdate with a child whose sibling has chicken pox.

Questions start to arise regarding screen time for children; what is the best age to get a child his own cell phone? The teen years bring new and even more frightening concerns: Help! My teenager is on the verge of learning to drive. Help! My teen is riding with new, inexperienced drivers.

From the moment you became a parent you've been driven to do everything in your power to make sure your child is safe and secure, healthy, happy and growing to become that well adjusted, responsible adult you dream of. This responsibility is daunting. You believe you must be vigilant.

However, your child does not have the same drive or quality world picture of being controlled by you, or anyone else. You may want your middle school child to complete her homework and continue to do well in school. You have a quality world picture of your daughter as the successful student you want her to be. But she may resist, focusing her energy and attention on her quality world pictures of horseback riding, or dance, or soccer, or training dogs. She tells you that she is perfectly satisfied with her present school performance. She is passing and that's good enough for her. She does not want to devote time to homework when there are more important things to do. Her quality world pictures are what's driving her.

Here is the difficulty. Parents spend much of their time trying to keep their children safe and alive. Children spend most of their time trying to meet their needs for love, power, fun and freedom. For many children who live in a secure and consistent world, the urge to feel safe is an afterthought. In fact, it may not even be a conscious thought or drive.

The parental challenge then is developing and maintaining a connected, responsible and respectful relationship with your children so you can have positive and effective influence over your child's choices. Your child does what you ask or suggest because he knows and believes you have his best interests at heart. Your child also knows when he wants something different from his parents' ideas, he can work with his parents to negotiate these differences.

Using Choice Theory pays off as your child gets older. She believes you will respect her and work with her as she learns new skills. She knows you will support her to achieve a responsible goal even if it is different from what you may want.

Your urge to control your child may **never** stop. My mother continued to worry and caution me about flying no matter how old I was. She was still my mother and still driven to keep me safe and alive. Despite your urge to control, start now to learn to manage this drive. Do not let your instinctive urge to control keep you from a life-long, loving connection with your child.

As long as you and your child maintain a connected, respectful relationship, you can offer your thoughts, ideas and suggestions in an attempt to influence your child's choices. But when you attempt to control, manipulate or insist your child do what you want using the external control strategies of criticism, threats, rewards, bribes and punishments, you run the risk of damaging your relationship. This also damages your ability to influence.

When you use threats like "clean your room or there will be no screen time later" or promise rewards such as, "study for your math test and we'll get ice cream" you both know what you're doing. You're trying to get her to do what you want even if it's not what she wants. These are obvious and easily recognizable attempts to try to control or manipulate your child.

Some other, more subtle attempts to control to change your child sound like this:
"Why do I have to ask you seven times before you put your back-pack away?"
"You are such a messy child!"
"You never do what you're asked!"
"I'm so disappointed in you! You know better than to act that way."
"You've embarrassed me in front of your teacher."

Parents say things to their children for the same reasons. They want their children to behave differently and hope by saying such things their children will change. Unfortunately the change that is more likely is the child feels less connected and loving toward his parent. Eventually he may begin to feel less love, pride and connection with himself.

Glasser called these the 7 Deadly Habits, deadly because of the potential damage to relationships. He also made a different list he called the 7 Caring Habits as alternative behaviors to help influence your child to behave differently.

7 Deadly Habits	7 Caring Habits
Criticizing	Supporting
Blaming	Encouraging
Complaining	Listening
Nagging	Accepting
Threatening	Trusting
Punishing	Respecting
Bribing or rewarding to control	Negotiating difference

Practice Tip

Identify and make a list of the ways you are currently attempting to overtly or covertly control your child's behavior, no matter your child's age. Refer to the list of deadly habits to help you identify what you are doing now.

Once you have your list, decide which of these behaviors you're willing to stop doing for one week — seven days.

When you have decided, keep a journal of what happens. What is this like for you? Do you notice any difference in your child? What are you doing every time you are tempted to return to your old ways? Remember, I'm not suggesting you stop this controlling behavior forever, simply for a week to see what you learn about yourself and learn about your child. Are you using a new and different but still externally controlling behavior? Are you leaving your child alone to figure it out for herself? Are you attempting to influence by giving a suggestion?

If you need help completing this tip, try re-reading this chapter again. What are you learning about your URGE TO CONTROL YOUR CHILD?

3. Why Do Kids Act That Way?

Key Points:

- *All behavior is purposeful.*
- *The purpose of all behavior is a child attempting to meet her needs for safety, love, power, fun and freedom*
- *Even though behavior is purposeful, it may not be effective*
- *Effective behavior may not be responsible or respectful.*
- *Responsible is the ability to meet your needs in ways that doesn't interfere with other people's ability to meet their needs.*
- *Respectful means the ability to meet your needs without attempting to power over another person.*
- *Parents need to teach their children how to meet all of their needs effectively, responsibly and respectfully*

Are you less concerned about why your child acts the way she does and more focused on getting her to STOP?

By now you should have a better understanding of your biological drive to protect your child which often turns into a strong urge to externally control her. This chapter is going to change your world. Really. This information is that important.

Your child's behavior is not your child's problem. Let that idea really sink in. When your child runs into the street, or stuffs his mouth with popcorn, or stays out well beyond his curfew, from the kid's point of view, his behavior is not a problem.

All behavior is purposeful. All behavior, from birth to death, is a person's best attempt to meet a need for safety, love, power, fun and freedom.

However, just because all behavior is purposeful does not mean that all behavior is effective, responsible, respectful, or following rules or laws. People do what they do because at the time it is the best choice available to them.

When a parent scolds her child for behaving rudely, it may not be the most effective or responsible choice, but at the time this parent is trying to teach her child manners. Reprimanding is not the way to help your child learn, but this mother isn't deliberately choosing an ineffective or disrespectful option and this is her quickest and best choice in this present moment.

The same is true for your child. Misbehaving children are choosing the best behaviors they know to get what they want and need. A three-year old wants to play with the family cat by pulling its tail, and engaging in rough play. His problem is he needs some fun and doesn't know any other way to get it with the cat. His father sees this behavior, and describes it as disrespectful, potentially dangerous and irresponsible. The father sees the problem as the child's behavior, but his child sees it differently.

Children do what they do because they don't know any other way to do it. It's the parents' job to teach their children to get what they need and want effectively and respectfully.

How do you do that? When parents scold, reprimand, threaten, punish or spank their misbehaving children it's because they don't know any other way to get their children to behave.

The best time to teach your child to behave respectfully and responsibly is when the child is actually misbehaving. This is when he will be most interested in learning some new behaviors, not because he is motivated to learn, but because he needs something immediately. He'll do whatever it takes to get what he wants, including learning something new.

Seize this as your moment to teach. Remember your child is doing what she is doing to get what she wants. Your job is to teach her how to do it differently and more effectively in a more acceptable way. Now you have a respectful well behaved child, just what you want!

You achieve this miracle by using the *magical questions*. Once your child learns this process he will use it effectively for the rest of his life.

Magical Questions

The next time your child misbehaves ask:

QUESTION 1: *What is it you want that you're trying to get by* _____? (Fill in the blank with whatever you see your child presently doing.

Example:

> a) *What is it you want that you're trying to get by hitting your brother?*
> b) *What is it you want that you're trying to get by screaming?*
> c) *What is it you want that you're trying to get by refusing to do your homework?*
> d) *What is it you want that you're trying to get by visiting a website we decided was off limits?*

This question is similar to asking your child *Why did you do that?* But you already know the universal answer to that question: *I don't know,* usually said with a shrug.

Please ask this question just this way, even though it is grammatically incorrect. When you do, your child will magically answer, at least most of the time.

(Those few times your child doesn't answer will be addressed later in this chapter.)

You've asked the question. You've received an answer (to the above questions):

a) That toy
b) I want chewing gum!
c) Free time to do what I want, not doing more school work now.
d) My friends told me there's something really cool on this website. I want to see.

QUESTION 2: *If we can figure out a way to help you get what you want and still follow the rules are you willing to learn how?* Some variations of this question include: *help you get what you want respectfully; or help you get what you want responsibly; or help you get what you want without hurting your brother or anybody else?*

Almost all of the time your child will answer yes. They don't care how they get what they want. They just want what they want and if it means behaving responsibly or within the rules they'll do it.

(What if your child says *no* they are not willing to learn a new way? We will address this later in the chapter as well.)

Work with your child to help him learn new, more effective ways to get what he needs and wants. Brainstorm with her as many alternative solutions as you both can think of. The brainstorming does not need to be limited to only responsible ideas. Brainstorming means all ideas are good and added to the list of alternative solutions. Once you have a variety of alternative solutions, help the child choose the responsible and best plan.

Using the examples above:

Here are some other ways you can get what you want:

> *a) Ask your brother to switch toys for a set time. Ask your brother to play a game with you. Find another toy you can use together to play a game.*

> *b) You could ask politely for chewing gum. You could wait until after lunch to ask for chewing gum. You would hold onto the gum without unwrapping it until all of your lunch is eaten then pop it into your mouth as soon as you're finished .*

> *c) You could rearrange your evening's schedule so you have the free time AND time to complete your homework. What ideas do you have of how you can make it work so you get the freedom you want and complete your homework?*

> *d) How can we work this out so you can go to the website in a responsible way? Do you have any ideas or suggestions? Let's figure this out together so you see what you want, and I know you're safe.*

When you understand that your child's behavior is not his problem, your own thinking shifts. Her problem is that there's something she wants and doesn't know how to get any other way. Now you understand that your job is to help your daughter learn to use responsible, respectful and effective behaviors to get what she wants.

I've labeled this process *magical*, because it works! Remember when your infant would cry and cry and cry? No matter what you did you couldn't stop the crying. At some point you probably said to your baby, *If you would only tell me what you want I can help.* Of course, then it didn't work.

But if you try it now you'll be astounded at the results! Now ask your crying and upset 2, 9, or 12-year old *What do you want that you're trying to get by crying and getting upset? Please tell me what you want and I'll help you get it.* Most of the time they will tell you, and most of the time you can help them figure out a better, more effective way to get what they want.

What If . . .

- Your child doesn't tell you what she wants:

What do you do when you ask your child what he wants and he doesn't tell you? If your child is a child and not a teenager, it may be that he doesn't know what he wants, or he is too young to use the words. Go ahead and ask the question a couple of times anyway. By asking, even if you don't get an answer, you are practicing for yourself, and teaching your son that this is a helpful question to ask when frustrated. If he is really young you can ask him to point to what he wants, but he may not understand that direction either.

- If you don't get an answer, guess. What do you think your child may want? Make a statement, rather than asking a question about what you guess your child wants.

When my children were toddlers and one was getting pushy and grabby with his brother I would ask, *"What do you want that you're trying to get by pushing and grabbing at your brother?"* After asking a couple of times I would make a statement of what I guessed he wanted. *"It looks like you want the toy truck and you're trying to get it from your brother by grabbing it and pushing him away. If we can figure out a way to help you get and play with your truck without hurting your brother, are you willing to work it out?"* Most times my guess was correct. Sometimes when my guess was wrong he would correct me. *No, I don't want the truck, I want to sit in that chair!* Ultimately if my guess was wrong, and my child wouldn't or couldn't tell me what he wanted I would state, *"When you can tell me what you want I'll be happy to help you get it respectfully."*

The other time when asking may result in silence is when your child is a teen. Among the things that teens want is privacy from their parents knowing what they want. Your teen has a greater need for power and freedom which will be discussed in Chapter 6. Keeping her desires and needs private helps her to meet her need for power and freedom. When you ask *"What do you want that you're trying to get by refusing to answer my question?"* she may not be willing to reveal herself to you at this time.

Still use the magical questioning process whether your child answers or not. But after you've asked once without any answer forthcoming, change your question into a statement, *"I know there's something that you want and that you're breaking a rule in an attempt to get it. What you may not know is I want to help you get what you want. I just want to help you learn to get what you want without breaking any rules and doing it irresponsibly. When you're ready to let me help you, let me know."*

Parenting teens is a lot like asking a cat to come when you call. Both may cooperate with you but only in their own time and when they are good and ready. Once you've made the above offer you may discover in a few days, while you and your child are doing something well removed from this latest conversation, that he may begin to tell you there's something he wants, and he needs your help getting responsibly. More magic!

When you've asked your child of any age if she's willing to learn a different, more respectful way to get what she wants and she says no, accept her answer. If she is doing something that is hurting or potentially hurting herself, others or property, remove her from the circumstances or remove the object from her reach. In other words, she cannot have whatever it is she wants until she learns to responsibly manage herself. Denial of access to the object or freedom is not punishment or forever. As soon as she is willing to learn to behave more responsibly she can have what she wants and your child determines when that is.

This is different from punishment in that you're thinking differently and changing your approach to your child. Can you see the differences?

"There's no more dessert for you until you can learn how to eat ice-cream politely."

Versus

"I understand you want to eat your ice cream in a messy, fun way. I'm happy to help you learn how to eat messy, fun and politely. When you're ready to learn let me know. . . "

And to answer those of you who are wondering how you create a messy, fun and polite way to eat ice cream, I don't have the answer. I am certain though, that if you accept that it's possible and present this challenge to your child, he will figure it out! As the parent, you don't need to know all the answers. You just need to be open to many possibilities and engage your child in using his imagination.

Please remember that just because your child has learned to be more responsible and respectful <u>this time</u> doesn't mean he won't fall back on his old habitual misbehaving choices. It's easier to push your way to the front of the line and be first to play with a new computer game rather than to negotiate for that spot or wait your turn. Learning new behaviors does not happen after the first try any more than learning to independently stand and walk happens right away for a pre-toddler.

This is a process you will use over and over and over again with your child. Eventually my children stopped grabbing a desired toy from his brother. Instead one boy would bring another desirable toy to his brother and negotiate a swap, sometimes asking me to set the timer for a future swap. Eventually my granddaughter asked me politely for an apple rather than whining and crying *I want an apple!*

Most amazing of all was when my sons became teenagers and started asking this question of me! *What is it you want Mom, that you're nagging to try and get? If we could figure out another way, are you willing to learn?* I was astonished, astounded, furious and delighted all at the same time. Not only were they using this process with and on me, they were using it to help them solve their own problems, not just alter misbehaviors.

I'm proud to say they continue to use this problem-solving process as adults, and as they parent their own children!

Learning this new way of parenting is challenging and requires patience, but it will change your life and the lives of your whole family for the better.

Practice Tips

- Start using the Magical Question Process now
- Write these questions on a file card and carry them with you for easy reference
- Use your journal to record how you and your child are doing following this process

4. Balancing Freedom and Safety

Key Points:

- *Parents want to keep their children safe.*
- *Children want freedom to explore the world and their abilities.*
- *There is an inherent tension between parents and children because of these conflicting needs.*

Is your child beginning to pull away from you? Perhaps you're trying to snuggle, hugging him for too long, or you kiss him farewell in public. When your 7-year old asks for her own cell phone, what do you answer? Do you have a plan for when your 12-year old declares that he and his friends are planning an overnight camping trip? Will you say yes when your 6-year old tells you she wants to walk alone to her friend's house for a play date? Is that the same answer you will give your 10-year old who says he wants to walk alone to the public library?

These are just some examples of the eternal conflicts between parent and child that begin before the child's birth. This biological conflict involves you pulling your kids close to keep them safe at the same time as they push away for more freedom.

Parenting peacefully means honoring your child's genetic need for more freedom, while you simultaneously teach her how to safely handle this freedom.

The balance between your needs and your child's is best achieved by slowly increasing allowable freedom while simultaneously teaching her how to remain safe. As infants grow, you provide greater freedom while ensuring they are in an enclosed and safe space. You patrol this space, making sure nothing is close at hand that might hurt your child or that your child might damage. You also make sure that some supervising adult is close if needed.

As your child gets older, the enclosed space increases in size and the adult supervision actually becomes greater, at least initially. Now your kiddo is more mobile and more able to get into more things that might hurt him or that he might harm. Luckily this is also just when your child begins to heed you when you say "No." Once your child follows your no direction you can increase his freedom from the constant supervision, but you still regularly check to be sure he remains safe.

You would never let your two-year old go out the front door alone. That is far too much freedom for your young child. It is equally absurd to keep a 16-year old inside of a playpen! Parents tend to over control their child at every age because they fear for the child's safety and well being.

If you are frightened of all the potential dangers your toddler or teen may encounter, start now to teach him how to responsibly handle them. Stop restricting or controlling your child so *you* feel safe. Your adolescent may obey your restrictive rules for the moment, but don't be surprised to learn later that she is disobeying you, going further afield than is permissible.

Helicopter parenting describes parents who provide too little freedom, who constantly hover. The result may be a child who complies but has no confidence or ability to manage and handle the simplest obstacles that confront him daily. You may end up with a young adult unable to manage independence; who is openly or secretly rebellious, or who disobeys, runs away, and takes extreme risks. This teen is desperately trying to meet her need for more freedom. The irony is that parents who control because of their fear for their child's safety are encouraging their child to lie, sneak and act out, putting them at greater risk. Both extremes, providing too little or too much freedom, does not help your child develop into an independent and capable adult.

If you want your children to make safe and responsible choices as teenagers, start by helping them learn how when they are younger. (Chapter 6 explains this in great detail.)

And so it goes . . .

I acted on and learned this advice when my children were 8-years old and I was making all the choices about their daily sugar consumption. I was following the rule my mother had for me when I was a child except I never knew how to implement it as the mother. The rules had been only one sweet treat a day, after a well balanced meal. But did this mean pancakes were a well balanced meal or a sweet treat? When offered a cookie after dinner at Nana's could they accept even though they had a different dessert after lunch earlier that day?

After a discussion with my husband, I announced a new plan to my children one spring morning. They were now in charge of their sweet consumption. Of course, my children could hardly believe their good luck! I told them I wanted them to tune into how they each felt if and when they ate too many cookies, or M&Ms, or plums, and we would check in after two weeks to see how they were doing. Initially they each over indulged, but eventually they managed their own balance of what and how much to eat of all foods, including sweets. There were a few times when I would interfere when one son went for another slice of birthday cake, but he was quick to point out that I had agreed to let him be in charge.

Later, when my children were teenagers and young adults facing different kinds of temptations, I worried much less. I knew they each had the necessary skills to face potentially dangerous choices that might be immediately rewarding but would ultimately lead to feeling unwell, sick and at risk.

Practice Tips

- Choose an area where you are presently making the choices for your child and start now by turning this over to her. It could be choosing her school clothes, her bedtime or the daily feeding the family dog. Ask her to be in responsible with this task. Does she need any help from you to learn how? Teach her what If she is unsure or needs help, teach her what she needs to know. Now she is in charge.

- Check in after a day or two and ask her to self-evaluate. How is she doing? Does she need any more help from you? Let her know you are ready and willing to be her helper or consultant, but you will not interfere as you see she is handling this her responsibility.

5. Safe Boundaries and Limitless Freedom

Key Points:

- *Slowly increase freedom as you teach responsible behaviors*
- *When your child demonstrates she has more freedom than she can handle responsibly, decrease the freedom only as long as it takes to teach new, responsible behaviors. Then reinstate the new freedom*

Do you remember helping your son learn to ride a bicycle? First you made sure he had the proper safety equipment: helmet, proper size bicycle, training wheels. Then you chose a safe area, like a bike path or park, where you could ride your bike together. You practiced, then practiced some more, giving instructions of what he needed to do to be a safe bike rider.

If he fell, you encouraged him get up and try again. Like the baby learning to stand, this process was repeated as many times as it took until he was confident and competent. You first gave him specified boundaries of where he could ride his bicycle, then increased and extended them as he demonstrated that he had the responsible behaviors to handle additional freedom.

Some freedoms require more serious and consequential decisions than others and are beyond the scope of this book. Taking you through an example of how you might manage this parental choice is beyond the scope of this book. (For individual coaching help please contact me: nancy@drnancybuck.com) But the process is the same whether you're helping your child learn to ride a bicycle, change to a later bed time, create expected curfews for week day and weekend outings, or taking your car out for the evening.

Parenting means supporting and helping your child increase her freedom responsibly. As you do this, whether it's virtually through the internet or in the real world, your child will be exposed to wonderful, scary, exciting, evil, limitless, glorious and immoral things. Trying to prevent this by restricting or imprisoning them is not effective, nor feasible and simply will not work. Your job is to help them recognize when they are putting themselves in vulnerable and potentially dangerous situations. Be the safe adult your children turn to for help, not the person they avoid telling things to, keeping secrets for fear of getting into trouble because they disobeyed or disappointed you.

I worry about my son who wants to walk to the library alone, my cab driver proclaimed when he learned I was a parenting expert. *My kid is good and responsible. It's all the crazy people out in the world I worry about.*

His is the concern of many parents. Your overwhelming desire is to protect your child from all potential hazards virtually and real.

But is this a practical solution? As my husband and I were discussing allowing our children to watch the old Disney film *Old Yeller*, one child ambled into the kitchen to tell us they had already watched that movie awhile ago at a friends house!

You cannot keep a thirsty person from seeking water, or a suffocating person from seeking air. And parents cannot keep their growing children from seeking new experiences and increased freedoms.

Instead, give your children the skills necessary to recognize danger. This is an ongoing parenting process for every age and stage of your child's development.

Find a class for parents of young children that teaches the skills necessary to teach and inform them about "Stranger Danger," available in most communities. Research if your community or your child's school offers classes on appropriate and safe school bus, play ground and classroom behavior. Does it include information about bullying? If not, request a course for parents and children. Discuss with your children what bullying looks and feels like. This should include adults who bully other adults or children. Sadly there are many examples of this: parents who attempt to bully sports coaches, coaches who bully children, teachers who intimidate, threaten and punish the children in the classroom. This is also when you can introduce and discuss the topic of cyberbullying, or people who use apps on their cell phones to bully others. If your child has a cell phone, check in frequently to discuss rules for safety and polite etiquette on the phone.

If applicable you can share situations where you've felt threatened by someone. What did you do? What are you frightened of now? Whose help do you seek? This should be a regular part of family discussions. Aim for balance. Discussing this daily is too frequent, and once a year is not enough. Help your children learn and know that they have the skills to keep themselves safe and protected.

Children of all ages need an adult they trust, who they can turn to when they are feeling threatened and unsafe. To be that person for your child ensures that you accurately and truthfully, share factual, and age appropriate information about these topics with them.

Practice Tips

- Observe areas where you are doing "for" your child. Is it time to teach her how to do it for herself?
- Observe areas where you are doing "with" your child. Is it time to teach him how to do it alone?

6. From Cooperation to Competition and Back Again

Key points:

- *Love and fun are the cooperating needs.*
- *Power and freedom are the competitive needs.*
- *A child's growth and development comprise alternating periods of cooperative stages followed by competitive stages.*
- *Children rely on love to feel safe and secure.*
- *Teens rely on power to feel safe and secure.*

You are probably aware of the *Terrible Twos*, even if your own child hasn't yet reached this stage. What exactly is happening with a strong-willed, contrary two-year old who refuses parental requests? One night you put your darling, fun and congenial son to bed and the next morning you discover an unrecognizable child who hates everything, stomping his foot, refusing all requests.

The idea of child development entails the predictable biological, psychological and emotional changes that occur in your child from birth, through adolescence, as he grows and progresses from dependency to increasing independence. Appreciating your child's developmental stages using Choice Theory psychology is very useful. It won't mean that your two-year old won't still go through the stage of declaring you are not the boss of her. But it does mean that your Choice Theory understanding can help you manage and cope better.

Remember that there are five psychological needs driving all behavior from birth to death. The needs of *love* and *fun* are cooperative; so your child needs a full repertoire of cooperating behaviors to effectively meet her needs for love and fun. *Power* and *freedom* are competitive needs, and your child needs to develop competitive behaviors to get these needs met.

Throughout childhood, children alternate between competitive and cooperative stages. The fifth need, the *survival* need drives your child to feel safe and secure. This is the stabilizing need, present during both the cooperative and competitive stages.

From birth until about age two years babies are mostly driven by their needs for love and fun. They smile and wave their arms in delight when they see you. They want to spend time with you, play peek-a-boo, and be held by you, not a stranger. Essentially, you and your baby are falling in love with one another, playing games, delighting in one another during this cooperative stage.

But then around age two a dramatic change occurs. Your wonderfully agreeable child starts demanding more freedom and more power. No! Me! Mine! Your darling is now practicing new competitive behaviors to help him better meet his need for power and control. Your job during this developmental stage is to provide as many alternatives as possible to help him do it. *Do you want water or juice? Do you want the green, pink or blue cup? Do you want to wear your striped, or rainbow pajamas?* Offering choices, when possible three choices, allows her greater freedom and power. However, this doesn't mean you are always able to offer choices. There will be times when you're in charge. Get creative. Come up with more ways to allow your child greater freedom and power. When you do this there will be fewer power struggles between you.

About six months after your child enters his competitive stage he will shift back into cooperative mode. Ahhh! Here is the child who wants to be with you, please you, and help you. Because he is so cooperative and less contrary you may begin to take these moments for granted. Don't! Enjoy these times while they last. It's during these phases he will be open to learning new behaviors to be successful. These are the best times to ask your son what additional freedom he would like to learn how to handle on his own. You can tackle this question together since during this stage he wants to connect with you.

About six months after entering a cooperative stage, your daughter will shift to another competitive stage, where she is driven for greater power and freedom. As before offer her more opportunities to be in charge and make even more choices. One mother allowed her 4-year old to plan the family menu every Thursday. Another father made one Saturday a month the day where his son was in charge and the boss, at least while they were at home.

This six month process of alternating between cooperative and competitive stages lasts until your child reaches age 7. Now the stages are longer, more like eight or nine months in each stage, but there is no exact timing for this. If it feels like you and your child are arguing, disagreeing, or engaged in push-pull battles more, there's a pretty good chance your child is in a competitive phase.

As frustrating as it feels having a child who wants to be in charge, it is essential for your child's successful growth and development. Your child needs to effectively learn to responsibly meet her needs for power and freedom. You want your 13-year old to be able to say no, standing in his own power to make good choices when peer pressure pushes him into dangerous areas. How will he know how to do that if he hasn't practiced and succeeded when he is 3 and 5 years old? Teaching and fostering your child's ability to handle ever increasing freedom and power means you are preparing him to confidently make good and safe choices when he is no longer under your constant supervision.

Parenting teens is different from parenting younger children. Teenagers are still driven by their need for belonging, but now they meet their needs by belonging to and with their friends. They still care about connecting with parents and family, but they don't want anyone to know this, including you. The same is true for their need for fun, only now they are more likely to tell you that you are not fun. They want to be with their friends for fun.

How your teen meets her competitive needs for power and freedom changes dramatically. She keeps her business private and secret. Although you may worry that she is involved in something dangerous, it's more likely that she is exercising this new way to meet her needs. Heeding the previous advice of slowly increasing and teaching new ways for your daughter to meet her needs for power and freedom sets you both up for greater success and effectiveness. You'll still worry, but you will learn to trust in her. You've been teaching her all along and you've learned that she has demonstrated good decision making prior to her teen years.

Safety and Security is Different for Children than Teens

During childhood when a child feels threatened and unsafe, even if he is in a competitive stage, he relies on cooperation, looking to you and other adults for safety. Remember how your two-year old behaved like a perfect angel when visiting the doctor only to turn around and demand her own way once you returned home? Your son didn't feeling safe with the doctor, but he knew he was secure enough with you to practice his new power and freedom seeking behaviors.

When teenagers feel unsafe, they rely on competitive behaviors. Teens push back against rule, boundaries and regulations. They are practicing new ways to be powerful and free from you and other authorities. Teens seek to push the rules at school to see how far they can get out of bounds before they get into trouble. This is part of normal development for adolescents.

Your job is to cooperate with your teen's need to compete. When a two-year old needed more power and freedom you provided more opportunities for her to choose her snack and the book to read before bedtime. Now that she is 14 you need to do the same thing in an age appropriate way. But how? With these choices and freedom there is greater risk. You're probably clear that you don't want to oppress you child so that you feel safe, but you're feeling stuck. The following process can help:

Do I Answer Yes or No?

- At this stage your teen may announce what he is going to do, rather than ask your permission. Follow the adage choose *your battles* and pretend he asked. That allows him to feel powerful and you to assume your guidance for safety is needed.

- Do you understand your child's request?

    Yes? Go on to the next step

No? Seek more information to be clear you know what your child is planning to do. For example, when my children asked to attend an overnight boy-girl party, I knew what I feared that meant! But I needed to ask to clarify. Turns out the first half of the party was co-ed. Then the girls went home and the boys stayed for a sleep over, and the entire party was chaperoned by parents.

- Does my child have the responsible behaviors necessary to handle this freedom?

    Yes? Go on to the next step.

    No? Take the time to teach the necessary responsible and effective behaviors. Don't go on to the next step until you're sure your child has the skills to handle the additional freedom. If that means you need more time than you have before the requested event occurs, your answer is still NO. Explain to your child that as soon as she can successfully demonstrate responsible behaviors your answer will change to YES. This may increase her incentive to learn quickly.

- What am I afraid of?

    If your answer is nothing, then go ahead and give your child permission to do whatever she is asking to do.

If you have specific fears can you create a plan for yourself to manage your fears while your child is engaged in his new freedom?

Do you need help or reassurance from your child to manage your fear? It's okay to tell your son what frightens you and ask if he can help you better manage this. Perhaps he can call you when he arrives at his destination and call you when he's about to leave for home, if appropriate. You might be surprised at your child's willingness help you. Let him know that you trust him, but could use a little help managing your fear without choosing greater restrictions or oppression as your way to cope.

If your fear is too great and you cannot manage any other plan then withhold your permission. Note that if you say no one time out of ten your child will not be happy but will probably respect your restrictions. However, if you say no nine times out of ten don't be surprised to learn that your child did not respect your boundaries.

- Follow-up with your child after the event. Ask her to self-evaluate how she managed this new freedom. Does she need your help with any unexpected obstacles she encountered? You should also take a turn self-evaluating how you manage your fears or concerns while she was out in the wider world without you.

Practice Tip

Take or make an opportunity to practice the above *Do I Answer Yes or No* process described above, even if it's only for a small issue. Practice now, when the request is less critical or fear-inducing. This will enable you to better manage yourself and your answers when your son's requests are more serious. He will also better understand the process so you can work together to provide him greater opportunities for unsupervised freedom.

7. You Can Predict the Future

Key points:

- *You already know your child's next dilemma.*
- *Plan now for successful intervention to avoid the future problem.*
- *Creating and following rules or regulations can eliminate regular sibling spats.*
- *Repeated failure is part of the journey to successful change.*

Every school day of my children's lives would find them walking through the back door striding to their bedrooms, dropping their back-packs anywhere along the way (usually in the path close to the back door) then quickly changing into their play clothes, grabbing a snack and dashing out the door again. Every day of my children's school lives I would remind, ask, nag, and then loudly proclaim, *Please put your back-pack away*, which meant into the coat closet. Eventually they would comply. The next day we would all repeat the same pattern.

At any point during my children's many years of attending school I could have predicted each child's behavior with his back-pack. I wasn't clairvoyant. We were all just mindlessly following the same irritating pattern.

What annoyances are predictable in your family life? There is undoubtedly a regular pattern that repeats accompanied by stress and irritation. Maybe it's how you all get out of bed and start your day. Or perhaps it's the bedtime routine. Do you have troubles getting your children to put away some article of clothing or clean their room? You know the next family tussle because it's just like the last one.

Here's how to approach this predictable tangle differently.

Choose a quiet, tension free time well removed from the problem area. Let your child know that you want to solve a problem with her. Describe the predictable pattern that you both engage in. Tell her what life would look like from your perspective if you and she were able to find an answer so there was no more problem.

For example, imagine I had followed my own advice and approached my son Paul differently at any time during his school years:

Paul, have you noticed that every day when you get home from school you drop your back-pack on the floor somewhere between the back door and the closet? And every day I ask, then nag, then lose my temper, shouting at you to put your back-pack away? Well, I'd like both of us to solve this problem. Let's figure this out together, ok?

You don't necessarily need an enthusiastic agreement here. You just want to avoid a clear protest or refusal. If he says NO, then let him know you want to work on this with him another time when he's ready and willing. But if he doesn't protest, even though he hasn't exactly said YES, proceed.

First I described how this part of the day would go if it was just as I wanted it to be. Then I asked him what it would be like for him if it was just what he wanted.

When you arrive home from school, I would love it if you would walk in the door, take 6 more steps and drop your back-pack on the floor of the closet. Then go upstairs to your bedroom and change into your play clothes. I'll have your snack ready for you when you come back down. That's what I want. How would you like it to be?

I don't know Mom. I really don't think about it. I just walk in and want to get changed as quick as I can so I can go outside and play basketball. I guess I could carry my back-pack another 6 steps to the closet. Do you really know that it's 6 steps?

I don't. Let's count it together. But before we count, do you want to guess how many steps it is?

(When possible engage in some kind of game or fun to help this problem solving process along. See CHAPTER 8 for more details.) He guessed it would be 10 steps. We count together and it turns out it's another 8 steps from the back door to the closet.

Do we have a new plan then?

Sure, I'll take another 8 steps when I get in the house and drop my back-pack in the closet before I go upstairs.

REMINDER: At first this new plan is probably going to fail. It's not that he's deliberately disobedient. He's just in the habit of doing what he's always done. If he follows his old pattern, don't say anything, just carry on as usual. If you want you could simply say *8 steps* as he follows his usual old pattern. **Remembering and honoring this may be the most difficult part of the process. Allow for and accept failure as part of the journey to success.**

Later that evening during a tension free time, perhaps after dinner, ask him to self-evaluate. How does he think he did with the new plan? You do not, and should not, evaluate how you think he did. But you also self-evaluate in front of him, telling him how you think you did.

I was proud of myself for not nagging or yelling. I was glad I only had to say '8 steps' and we both knew what that meant.

Finally ask him if there is any change he thinks is needed to make the plan successful. I might also say, *Paul would it help if I reminded you 8 steps just as you come in the door? Is that a modification we should make to the plan?*

Not really Mom. When you nag me then I don't want to do the plan. It's okay if you want to say '8 steps' afterward if I forget though.

Repeat the plan again the next day, and both of you self-evaluate again. Any need to modify or change the plan? Repeat, as many times as it takes until you are successful.

There is no predicting how many times you will experience failure, self-evaluation, need for modification or not, and then repetition until you finally succeed. You are learning and creating a new habit. This process will probably take longer than you want it to, but not as long as you fear it will take. Your patient and positive attitude with your child throughout this process says to your child that you are both aiming for a unified goal and you will work together as long as it takes to successfully achieve your target. Too often the reason this process fails is because parents give up. One attempt with one failure, followed by another attempt with another failure can discourage parents into quitting. Don't let that happen. Expect the failures knowing that together you will both succeed. Once you give up, your children give up too. Begin this process knowing you will work together for as long as it takes until you solve the problem together.

This same process can be used when there is conflict between siblings. Instead of you and your child working to solve the problem, you ask your children to sit with you and you function as the coach. You start by describing the problem as you see it. Then ask each to describe how life would be for him or her if the problem was solved. You then facilitate everyone brainstorming   possible solutions. However, solutions such as Johnny telling Jane what she needs to do to solve the problem are off limits. They need to brainstorm their own behavior change. You can also suggest ideas for the list you're creating. Once a good list is made, help them work together until they arrive at a specific plan that both agree will solve the problem. Each commits to what he or she is going to do.

Remember, there will be hiccups when starting the new plan. Spend time asking each person to self-evaluate. Intervene if necessary when one child wants to blame the other for lack of success in following the new plan. Self evaluation means that each person evaluates himself or herself only, not the other. Each gets to make suggestions for modifying or changing the plan but only identifying what they themselves can do. Try again. You coach if and when necessary. The process is completed when they have successfully implemented the new plan enough times so that it has become the new habit.

RULES or REGULATIONS

Not every predictable friction calls for an individualized problem solving session. You can often resolve the regular squabbles between or among your children by creating fair and equitable rules.

Often these spats arise when you request some help or participation in household tasks.

Here are some examples from my family:

1. The dishwasher rule was that each boy would empty and put the clean dishes away. The original "rule" was that Paul would empty the top shelf, David would empty the bottom shelf for a month and then they would switch. This rule changed after Paul stated he always wanted the dishes on the top shelf because it was the easier shelf and David was happy to go along with this because he thought the dishes on the bottom were easier. Their modification became the new rule.

2. On an index card I wrote the letter P on one side, the letter D on the opposite side. This card was posted on the refrigerator. When it was time to empty the kitchen garbage bag into the larger bin in the garage, I would call upon the child whose initial I read on the refrigerator card. When their job was done he would turn the index card over so his brother's initial was now visible. The next time the opposite child would be called on to help out. One time David forgot to flip the card over. When his name was called again he protested and pleaded with me, declaring it wasn't really his turn. I reminded him of the rule that I was following by naming the

child whose initial appeared on the card. He
never again forgot to flip the card over.

Practice Tips

- Choose a   predictable area of friction between
  you and your child. If possible choose the least
  challenging problem to start with. With your child
  now plan how you will work together and
  successfully resolve this ongoing problem.
- Choose an area of conflict between your children
  and coach them to successfully resolve their
  conflict.
- As a family, create rules or regulations to resolve
  or eliminate the predictable bickering battles
  between or among your children.

8. The Secret Strategies for Successful Parenting

Key Points:

- *Fun*
- *Unconditional and unchanging LOVE*

Every parent can learn and use the secret strategies that invite, entice, and encourage your children to do almost anything you ask. This may sound manipulative, like a strategy to externally control them, but you'll be using this secret out in the open. It won't really be a secret at all.

All children are born with the need for fun and they will do almost anything to meet this need. You probably know what I mean if you've ever taken your child to a church service. The kiddo will figure out how to make it fun, sometimes in a loud or disrespectful way. No one, no matter their age, ever stops being driven to meet their need for fun. It's just that children feel and follow this urge more readily than adults. One of the wonderful benefits of living and spending time with children is that they remind you that you need fun too.

The secret strategy for parents is to sprinkle fun into your requests or demands as often as you can. Remember in Chapter 6 when I asked Paul to count the actual number of steps between the back door and the coat closet? I was introducing a fun guessing game into the process of solving a problem. Not every request or chore needs to include fun. But it's just "funner" when there's fun. It's also more likely your children will do what you ask without complaint.

Asking my children to go to bed found them dawdling and continuiing to do whatever it was that they were already involved in. When I turned my request into a game they jumped up ready and willing to play. We created a contest to see who could get into PJs with teeth brushed and into bed first, the two of them or me. My sons did not suddenly get interested in going to bed, but they were always ready to play. It wasn't that they wanted to go to bed, they just wanted to have a race!

(Please note I did not ask them to compete against each other. They were already competing against one another in a competitive stage. Instead they teamed up to compete against me.)

When it's time to clean up a play area, you can ask your children to put away all of the toys with wheels, then all of the red toys, then all of the toys with a face, and so forth. Your children will go along with the plan, not because they care about cleaning up or putting things away. They just can't resist playing a game.

Several years ago while I was watching an in depth story about an Olympic athlete, the young man's father was explaining that his son had always been competitive. This Dad shared that when he was frustrated with his inability to get this child to drink his milk, the father poured himself a glass of milk too and then challenged his son to see who could drink the contents of the glass the fastest. This father turned his request into a game and the child couldn't resist playing the game.

Are you worried that you're lacking the creative skills necessary to come up with the games necessary to cover all potential events? You don't need to be the only game creator. Ask your children to invent a good game everyone can play while you complete a boring or unpleasant chore. The kids will do it! Some of these games may have intricate and complicated rules to follow. Don't worry. The child who is in the competitive stage will love being the boss and the referee, keeping everyone in line following these rules!

REMINDER: Even when you make the request or task fun, your children still won't necessarily drop what they're in the middle of and do as you ask. Insisting that they should do as you ask when you ask it of them is potentially damaging to your relationship. Asking for their help, giving them opportunity to complete what they are doing before you asked means you are being reasonable and respectful toward them.

Here's a word of advice for those of you presently parenting teens. One of the ways teens like to have fun is to let you know that you're no fun. Being willing to laugh at yourself along with your teen helps both of you. Teens are also more willing to go along with the game if they have younger siblings. This emerging adult is able to show his sophistication by telling you that he's only playing to help out his younger cousin or sister.

This secret about fun can also work for you. Do you have a regular chore that you dread? Turn it into a game! One woman told me she cleaned each room of her house as if it was an Olympic event. How long did it take for her to clean her sitting room last week? Can she clean it in less time this week? Another fellow told me that he mowed the grass in his yard following different patterns as a way to entertain himself during this chore.

Foolproof Parenting Plan

The father of a six-year-old first grader was concerned because Charlie, his gentle, easygoing, friendly son had befriended a classroom bully. The bully, a larger child than the others in his class, did not bully or attempt to control Charlie. But the bully did prevent all of the other children from getting too close or becoming friends with Charlie. This child wanted to keep Charlie to himself. Charlie's parent were considering taking him out of the school and sending him to another. *What should he and his wife do?*

To better understand this situation, I asked for more information. Was Charlie unhappy with this friendship? Did Charlie feel as if he was being isolated from other children he might want to play with or make friends with? Or was Charlie the type of kind and sympathetic child who saw this other child's isolation and sought him out? If that was the case, it was more than likely that sending Charlie to another school would only result in Charlie finding the isolated bully-like child in that class. Did Charlie have an opportunity to play with other children at some time during his school day and on weekends? During class times, did the teacher help Charlie pair with other children? Did the teacher pair the "bully" with other children? Had Charlie's parents had any conferences or conversations with this teacher? Had they had any conversations with Charlie?

As it turned out, Charlie's parents had discussed the situation with Charlie's teacher. *She's a very experienced, seasoned teacher,* his father told me. *She really seemed to understand immediately, sharing with us that she had observed what we were talking about. She also reassured us that she would continue to monitor the situation and intervene appropriately.*

Perhaps you can relate. With each passing year our children are maturing and growing. They are becoming increasingly independent from us. Will they be okay? Are they prepared? Have we done all we can to help them? Are we doing enough? Are we doing too much?

Parenting our children is a hard job, isn't it? I asked this father.

It really is, he admitted to me with relief. *It's much harder than I ever thought. I was the youngest of my parents' six children. How did they do it?*

Now we were at the heart of this father's worries and concerns. As parents, you want to do the best job you can for your children. But what does that mean? How do you know what is best? Will it be too late if you realize what you have done may not have been the best for your child?

So, here it is, the absolute foolproof plan for successful parenting that all parents are already capable of implementing. (Cf. Buck, Nancy. How To Be A Great Parent, New York, NY. Beaufort Books, 2013.) If you follow this advice, I guarantee it will help you and your child. Ready?

Step 1: *Every day tell your child that you love her.* When you see her for the first time in the morning wish her a good morning and tell her you love her. When you bid her good-bye as you each go off to your daily routine, tell her you love her. When you greet her again in the evening, smile and tell her that you love her. When you tuck her in bed at night, wish her good night and tell her that you love her. Smile from your heart and generously share your love for her in word and deed. For a few moments during the day and evening when you are apart, conjure up your child's beautiful face and remember that you love her.

Step 2: *Every day, laugh and play often.* Take time out and get away from all the important adult tasks on your to-do list. Instead, put these things aside during your day, evening and weekend and play a silly game, read a good book — do something together! Laugh and play with your child lots and lots and lots.

By doing these seemingly simple things you are helping your child meet her ever so important needs for love, power, fun and freedom. In fact, you're both meeting your needs together enhancing your bond and connection.

Too many of us grew up following our parents' admonition, *You can't go and play until you get all of your chores done.* As children, most of us were capable of completing our chores with time left over to play. Now, as an adult, are you waiting to play with your child until you get your work done? Don't wait. You will never get all of your work done. But your child will not be a child forever. He is not going to be waiting around for you to get your chores done. Instead, laugh and play with him now, then complete some of your work. Play now.

Ten years after your child has left home, you won't even remember what chore or work was so important. Spend time now laughing, playing a game, singing a goofy song. If you do, ten years after your child leaves home, you both will remember your time of love, laughter and play.

That is the complete, absolute, foolproof plan for successful parenting. Can you do it? Of course you can! Will you do it? I hope so.

Practice Tip

Complete both tip 1 and 2 every day this week

9. What's Next?

Key Points:

- *Accept and celebrate your child exactly as she is now.*
- *Neither parenting nor childhood is a competition.*
- *Cultivate gratitude and celebration.*

The solution of adult problems tomorrow depends upon the way we raise our children today. There is no greater insight into the future than recognizing when we save our children, we save ourselves .

Margaret Mead

As parents we all possess that urge to improve our children by "controlling" and "changing" our children for improvement. We are not primarily driven by our thirst to control. Rather, we all want our children to live, to be healthy, happy and successful. Surely our own ego and pride also plays a part in the equation; raising children to become good, kind and moral adults reflects well on us. But mostly we want our children to make good choices and be good people.

We've discussed at length the perils associated with attempting to externally control our children so they will become the kind of people we want. When our goal is always to develop and maintain a mutually respectful, loving relationship, we then have a positive influence on who our children are who they will become.

But along the way there are parents who, like the grandmother who phoned me all those many years ago, want to change *one little problem* about their child.

> *My daughter is a messy, never putting her things away.*
>
> *My son doesn't seem to take responsibility for his things.*
>
> *My daughter dawdles and is day dreaming all the time when I want her to listen.*
>
> *My son is a night owl. I can't get him to bed or sleep before midnight, then getting him up in the morning is a battle.*
>
> *Will my children ever be friends with each other? They bicker and argue all the time.*

Much of this book has been about how to address these kinds of problems in a different, more effective way. But there's also another important strategy to keep in mind that isn't unique to Choice Theory psychology: Gratitude.

Express your gratitude for the wonderful person your child is in this present moment. Celebrate her uniqueness. Get curious and consider how these seemingly annoying qualities might actually serve her well. Give thanks for your wonderful child just exactly the way he is right now.

Who might your child might become? Won't it be wonderful to spend your time together discovering just how these qualities will evolve? Who knows what talents and strengths are hidden beneath what you presently consider to be unwanted or impractical personality trait?

A messy child might become someone who mashes and synthesizes ideas, or arrives at a new chemical a formula.

A strong willed child might become a community organizer with clear vision and the drive needed to make this vision a new reality.

A day dreaming child might become a playwright or music composer.

None of us has any idea of how what we presently perceive to be a negative trait or inclination could evolve into a gift and talent.

In general only intervene or try to influence behavior when your child behaves irresponsibly, doing or saying something that interferes with other's abilities to meet their needs. And if your child's expressed uniqueness is interfering with the families' ability to accomplish an agreed upon goal, then work together to solve that problem.

But if your child is expressing her unique personality responsibly and it's not interfering with the family functioning, you can shift your thinking from worry or annoyance to celebration! Keep your opinions and judgements about your idea of a different, more perfect child to yourself. Understand that your child is perfect NOW, even if this perfection is different from what you imagined. Instead observe who your child actually is. Allow yourself to be introduced to and delighted by this person your child is. Look for all that there is to celebrate!

Cultivate a family environment filled with plenty of safety, security and freedom. This allows everyone to be his or her own unique self where freedom of expression, growth and evolution is possible. Who knows who your child can and will become in such an environment? Who knows what kind of accepting, loving and proud parent you can become?

I have a hunch that many parental complaints reflect the unspoken yet prevalent   culture of intense competition, at least in the United States. Some parents, as soon as they learn they are pregnant, immediately register their unborn child with the best preschools said to have the highest standards. Parents want their children to win. But childhood is not a competition.

And some parents act as if parenting too is a competition. However, you are only in a struggle with your mother-in-law, sister or your best friend over who can raise the best kid if you choose to think you are. Parenting is challenging and difficult enough without adding this pressure to the mix.

The obvious result of asking children and parents to compete to be the best (whatever that means) is a society filled with stressed, anxious and depressed children and parents. This book offers you different and better strategies to prevent you from falling into this trap.

There is no such thing as a *perfect* or even *best* parent. Instead aim to be a conscious parent. The first step toward being a peaceful parent, a great parent or a conscientious parent is to be conscious -- aware of what you are doing and why you are doing it. Why are you doing what you do? Are you doing things a certain way because that's what your parents did? Do you agree with these choices? You can parent differently or exactly the same, but first you need to be conscious of what you are doing. You don't even have to parent each of your own children the same way. Your last child may have greater freedom than your first child because you've learned how to manage this process better with each subsequent child. In order to make more effective parenting choices in the future, you first need to be conscious of the choices you're presently making. When you consciously acknowledge what you want and how you are getting there, you became an effective parent rather than a stressed and self-critical one.

Practice Tip

Take a time-out regularly for yourself. A daily time-out is best because of all the many things you're trying to accomplish every day. But if daily is too difficult, then do it at a minimum weekly. Spend this time self-reflecting, in writing if you choose, or just in thought. How are you doing? What did you do as a parent this week that you're proud of? What is the most important parenting change you want to make now? Are you hugging your children daily? Are you telling them that you love them? Do you play with them daily, even if it's a brief game of *I Spy*, especially with your teenagers.

Are you noticing all the ways your are positively learning and growing into a more effective parent? Are you and your children meeting your needs responsibly and respectfully every day? Are you staying connecting during the challenging times as well as the fun, agreeable times? Celebrate!

Resources

The purpose of this book is to help you learn and apply Choice Theory psychology to parenting. This brief book is certainly not exhaustive on the subject. But I hope I have given you enough information to begin using these ideas on your own parenting journey now. For more I would recommend that you refer to my other parenting books:

How To Be A Great Parent: Understanding Your Child's Wants and Needs, Dr Nancy S Buck, Beaufort Books, New York, NY, 2013.

Why Do Kids Act That Way? The Instruction Manual Parents Need to Understand Children at Every Age. Nancy S Buck, PhD. self-published, 2009.

Peaceful Parenting Workbook, Nancy S Buck, PhD. self-published, 2009.

Please read all of the books written by William Glasser, MD. He offers you great learning on Choice Theory psychology from the master himself.

The Choice Theory in Action Series Titles

A Choice Theory Psychology Guide to Addictions: Ways to Overcome Substance Dependence and Other Compulsive Behaviors - Michael Rice

A Choice Theory Psychology Guide to Anger Management: How to Manage Rage in Your Life - Brian Lennon

A Choice Theory Psychology Guide to Depression: Lift Your Mood - Robert E. Wubbolding, Ph.D.

A Choice Theory Psychology Guide to Happiness: How to Make Yourself Happy - Carleen Glasser

A Choice Theory Psychology Guide to Parenting: The Art of Raising Great Children - Nancy S. Buck Ph.D.

A Choice Theory Psychology Guide to Relationships - Kim Olver

A Choice Theory Psychology Guide to Stress: Ways of Managing Stress in Your Life - Brian Lennon

The Choice Theory in Action Series is available from Amazon as e-books or paperbacks and may be obtained through bookshops including wglasserbooks.com

William Glasser International

The body that Dr. Glasser approved to continue teaching and developing his ideas is William Glasser International.

This organization helps coordinate the work of many member organizations around the world.

WGI recently introduced a six-hour workshop entitled, "Taking Charge of Your Life". This is intended for the general public and provides a good foundation in Choice Theory psychology.

If you are interested in further training in Choice Theory psychology or any of its applications, you are recommended to contact WGI or your nearest member organization of WGI.

www.wglasserinternational.org

Made in the USA
Coppell, TX
21 January 2021

48578200R00049